PLANET UNDER PRESSURE
ENERGY

Clive Gifford

www.raintreepublishers.co.uk

Visit our website to find out more information about **Raintree** books.

To order:
- ☎ Phone 44 (0) 1865 888113
- 📄 Send a fax to 44 (0) 1865 314091
- 💻 Visit the Raintree bookshop at
www.raintreepublishers.co.uk
to browse our catalogue and order online.

First published in Great Britain by Raintree, Halley Court, Jordan Hill, Oxford OX2 8EJ, part of Harcourt Education.
Raintree is a registered trademark of Harcourt Education Ltd.

© Harcourt Education Ltd 2006
The moral right of the proprietor has been asserted.

Editorial: Sarah Shannon and Louise Galpine
Design: Lucy Owen and Bridge Creative Services Ltd
Picture Research: Natalie Gray and Sally Cole
Production: Chloe Bloom

Originated by Repro Multi Warna
Printed and bound in China by South China Printing Company

ISBN 1 844 43978 X
10 09 08 07 06
10 9 8 7 6 5 4 3 2 1

British Library Cataloguing in Publication Data
Gifford, Clive
Energy. – (Planet under pressure)
333.7'913

A full catalogue record for this book is available from the British Library.

Acknowledgements
The publishers would like to thank the following for permission to reproduce photographs: Alamy pp. **6–7** (Rod Howe), **24–25** (Tina Manley); Corbis pp.**18–19, 32–33;** Corbis pp. **16–17; 36–37** (Andrew Wong); Corbis/Owaki-Kulla pp. **26–27;** Digital Vision/Harcourt Education Ltd pp.**12–13, 22–23;** Ecoscene pp. **22–23** (Peter Hulme); Empics pp. **29, 32–33** (Kazuhiro Nogi); Getty Images/PhotoDisc pp. **8–9;** Lonely Planet pp.**10–11** (Richard l'Anson); Panos pp. **10–11** (Caroline Penn), **20–21, 40–41** (Mark Henley); Reuters pp. **30–31;** Science Photo Library pp. **28–29** (Vanessa Vick), **38–39** (Martin Bond); Science Photo Library/EFDA-JET pp. **40–41;** Science Photo Library/US Dept. of Energy pp.**16–17;** Still Pictures pp. **14–15** (S Compoint), **34–35** (Hartmut Schwarzbach), **36–37** (Mark Edwards).

Cover photographs of dam with water flowing and of Times Square, New York reproduced with kind permission of Getty.

Every effort has been made to contact copyright holders of any material reproduced in this book. Any omissions will be rectified in subsequent printings if notice is given to the publishers.

The paper used to print this book comes from sustainable resources.

Contents

**Any words appearing in the text in bold,
like this, are explained in the Glossary.**

Energy use around the world

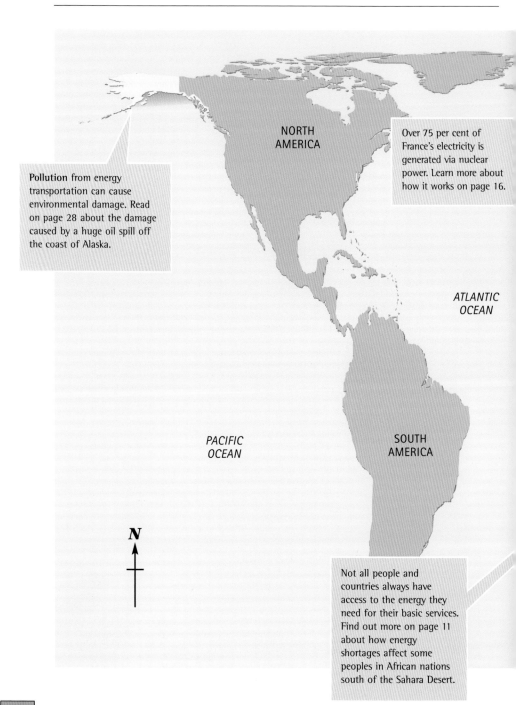

NORTH
AMERICA

Over 75 per cent of
France's electricity is
generated via nuclear
power. Learn more about
how it works on page 16.

Pollution from energy
transportation can cause
environmental damage. Read
on page 28 about the damage
caused by a huge oil spill off
the coast of Alaska.

ATLANTIC
OCEAN

PACIFIC
OCEAN

SOUTH
AMERICA

N

Not all people and
countries always have
access to the energy they
need for their basic services.
Find out more on page 11
about how energy
shortages affect some
peoples in African nations
south of the Sahara Desert.

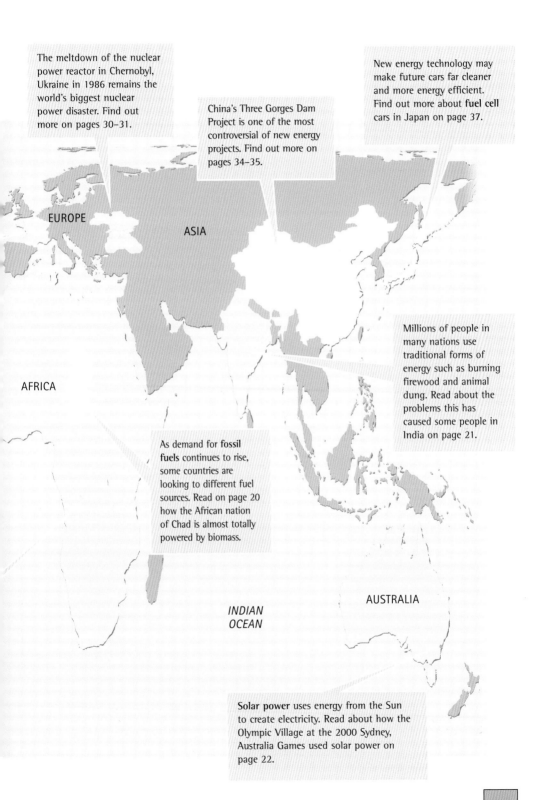

The meltdown of the nuclear power reactor in Chernobyl, Ukraine in 1986 remains the world's biggest nuclear power disaster. Find out more on pages 30–31.

China's Three Gorges Dam Project is one of the most controversial of new energy projects. Find out more on pages 34–35.

New energy technology may make future cars far cleaner and more energy efficient. Find out more about **fuel cell** cars in Japan on page 37.

EUROPE

ASIA

AFRICA

Millions of people in many nations use traditional forms of energy such as burning firewood and animal dung. Read about the problems this has caused some people in India on page 21.

As demand for **fossil fuels** continues to rise, some countries are looking to different fuel sources. Read on page 20 how the African nation of Chad is almost totally powered by biomass.

AUSTRALIA

INDIAN OCEAN

Solar power uses energy from the Sun to create electricity. Read about how the Olympic Village at the 2000 Sydney, Australia Games used solar power on page 22.

The demand for energy

Everything we do, from taking a bus to turning on a tap, and everything we consume, from a fizzy drink to the clothes we wear, requires energy. Energy is necessary to produce goods, package them, move them around, use them, and dispose of them. Energy is essential for providing heating, lighting, transport, and many other things which form part of our everyday lives.

What is energy?

Energy is the ability to do work and is found in many different forms. It is all around us in the forms of heat and light energy given out by the Sun. There are vast amounts of energy in the movement of tides and waves, and chemical energy is found and stored in substances such as oil and coal. Energy cannot be created or destroyed, but it can be transformed from one type to another. For example, your body's muscles store a form of chemical energy which is transformed into moving or "kinetic" energy when you move a part of your body.

   Converting energy into forms which can be used to provide heat, light, and power is of vital importance to the world's human population. For example, when a substance such as oil or coal is burned, it releases large amounts of heat energy. This heat energy is used in industry to melt and extract valuable metals from rocky **ores**. It can also be used to fuel a power station which converts the heat energy into electricity.

Statistics

A 40-Watt lamp light bulb switched on for an hour uses 0.04 kWh of power. It takes over 3,750 times as much electricity to produce a single kilogram of the metal aluminium.

The energy industry

Supplying energy in convenient and useful forms to people and businesses is the role of the energy industry. It is one of the world's biggest industries, worth over £30 billion in the United Kingdom alone, where it employs more than 200,000 people. These figures are dwarfed by the United States which spends approximately US$450 billion per year on energy. A large section of the energy industry is devoted to generating and supplying electricity.

Top 20 electricity consuming nations in 2001

1.	USA	3,602,000 million kWh
2.	China	1,312,000 million kWh
3.	Japan	964,200 million kWh
4.	Russia	773,000 million kWh
5.	Germany	506,800 million kWh
6.	Canada	504,400 million kWh
7.	India	497,200 million kWh
8.	France	415,300 million kWh
9.	UK	346,100 million kWh
10.	Brazil	335,900 million kWh
11.	Italy	289,100 million kWh
12.	South Korea	270,300 million kWh
13.	Spain	210,400 million kWh
14.	Mexico	186,700 million kWh
15.	Australia	184,400 million kWh
16.	South Africa	181,200 million kWh
17.	Ukraine	152,400 million kWh
18.	Taiwan	140,500 million kWh
19.	Sweden	134,900 million kWh
20.	Poland	118,800 million kWh

Source: CIA World Factbook 2003

Electricity

In little more than a century, electricity has gone from being a scientific curiosity to the most common form of everyday energy. Electricity has many advantages. It can be easily transmitted from a power station by power cables to individual homes, offices, and locations. It can be converted relatively easily into heat energy, mechanical energy, or to power electronic devices and it can be controlled instantly, with a single switch.

Average electricity use of typical household appliances in USA

	Energy use per hour (kWh)	Hours use per year	kWh per year
Electric oven and hob	12.200	96	1,171
Microwave oven	1.450	131	190
Dish washer	1.201	302	363
Toaster	1.146	34	39
Coffee maker	0.894	119	106
Hair dryer	0.750	51	38
Vacuum cleaner	0.630	73	46
Refrigerator-freezer – 14 ft^3 frostless	0.615	2,974	1,829
Washing machine (automatic)	0.512	208	107
Colour TV	0.300	2,200	197
Clock	0.002	8,760	17

Source: University of Nebraska-Lincoln, 2002

Total world energy use in billions of barrels of oil equivalent

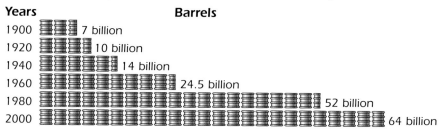

Years	Barrels
1900	7 billion
1920	10 billion
1940	14 billion
1960	24.5 billion
1980	52 billion
2000	64 billion

Oil is frequently measured in units called barrels. One barrel is equal to 159 litres (42 US gallons). The energy in one barrel of oil is equivalent to approximately 400 kg (881 lb) of coal.

Source: US Department of Energy

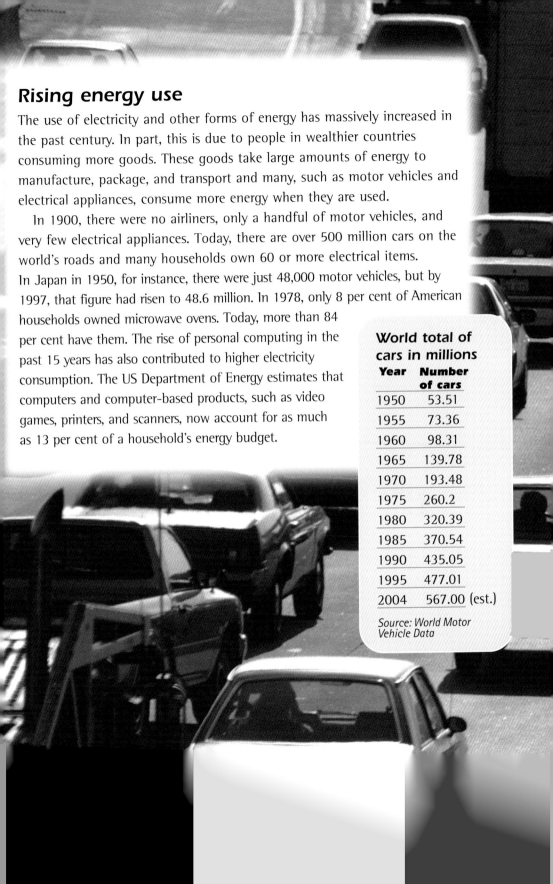

Rising energy use

The use of electricity and other forms of energy has massively increased in the past century. In part, this is due to people in wealthier countries consuming more goods. These goods take large amounts of energy to manufacture, package, and transport and many, such as motor vehicles and electrical appliances, consume more energy when they are used.

In 1900, there were no airliners, only a handful of motor vehicles, and very few electrical appliances. Today, there are over 500 million cars on the world's roads and many households own 60 or more electrical items. In Japan in 1950, for instance, there were just 48,000 motor vehicles, but by 1997, that figure had risen to 48.6 million. In 1978, only 8 per cent of American households owned microwave ovens. Today, more than 84 per cent have them. The rise of personal computing in the past 15 years has also contributed to higher electricity consumption. The US Department of Energy estimates that computers and computer-based products, such as video games, printers, and scanners, now account for as much as 13 per cent of a household's energy budget.

World total of cars in millions

Year	Number of cars
1950	53.51
1955	73.36
1960	98.31
1965	139.78
1970	193.48
1975	260.2
1980	320.39
1985	370.54
1990	435.05
1995	477.01
2004	567.00 (est.)

Source: World Motor Vehicle Data

Population boom

A major proportion of the massive increase in energy use is due to the explosion in the world population. In 1750, there were 791 million people on the planet. By 1950, there were 2,500,000,000 and today, there are 6,400,000,000 people.

The majority of the planet's people live in countries such as China, India, and Brazil, which are developing their industries and economies to match the nations of the developed world.

In many developing countries, energy use is rising rapidly as populations increase and people consume more goods. Access to electricity is improving and more people can afford to buy cars and other energy-using appliances. Between 1981 and 2000, for example, the amount of electricity used per person in rapidly developing countries in South-east Asia, including Malaysia and South Korea, increased by 232 per cent.

As the demand for energy rises massively, it creates major pressures on the planet and the life it supports. As the later chapters of this book show, many energy sources generate harmful pollution, waste, and other environmental problems. For many of the world's people, though, their biggest problem with energy is obtaining enough of it. Energy either costs too much or is not available in their regions. Over a quarter of the world's people do not have regular access to electricity.

Stripping the land for energy

In many African countries south of the Saharan desert, people rely on gathering firewood as their energy source for heat and cooking.
In some regions, this has resulted in the land being stripped of tree cover. Women and children, especially, are forced to scour the land for many hours every day just to collect enough wood for a small fire. For many people living in these regions, cold or raw food is a daily reality.

Renewable and non-renewable energy

Some energy sources are **renewable**. This means they can be used over and over again as they are continually being replaced. Examples of renewable energies are wind, wave, and solar power. But the most-used energy sources of all – oil, coal, and **natural gas** – are all non-renewable. These cannot be replenished at anything close to the rate they are being used (see pages 14–15). Reserves of some non-renewable energies in some countries are close to being exhausted (see page 15).

What you can do to save electricity

- Investigate your own room and then your home to see how many electrical items have a plug and require electricity from the mains. Ensure all items not in use are unplugged.
- Switch off lights when you leave a room.
- Replace regular light bulbs with energy-saving models (see page 39).

Powering the planet

The world population's use of energy is enormous and continually increasing. All sorts of energy sources are used but oil, coal, and gas are the most important. They provide over 80 per cent of all the energy used by the world's population.

Fossil fuels

Coal, oil, and natural gas are called "fossil fuels" as they are created from the dead remains of animals and plants. Over millions of years, these remains have been covered by layers of silt, mud, and other sediment which eventually form rock in which fossil fuels are present. Fossil fuels can either be burned or be transformed into electricity; fossil fuels are used to generate almost two-thirds of the world's electricity.

COAL

Coal was the first of the fossil fuels to be used heavily in industry and by 1910, it accounted for almost 60 per cent of the world's energy use. Today that figure has fallen to a little over 20 per cent but this still means that over 4,580 million tonnes of coal are mined every year. Coal is used both in industry as a fuel for furnaces and to generate electricity in thousands of coal-fired power stations. Coal deposits are found all over the world, sometimes close to the surface where giant open cast mines are created, or deep underground where they can only be reached through deep mineshafts. Today, China is the world's biggest consumer of coal, using around 30 per cent of the world's coal every year. It is also the world's biggest producer.

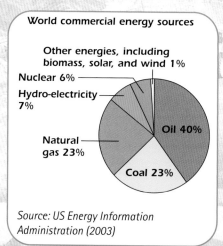

World commercial energy sources

Other energies, including biomass, solar, and wind 1%
Nuclear 6%
Hydro-electricity 7%
Natural gas 23%
Oil 40%
Coal 23%

Source: US Energy Information Administration (2003)

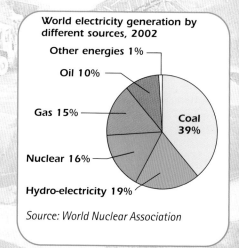

World electricity generation by different sources, 2002

Other energies 1%
Oil 10%
Gas 15%
Coal 39%
Nuclear 16%
Hydro-electricity 19%

Source: World Nuclear Association

OIL

Crude oil is a naturally occurring substance found trapped in certain rocks below the Earth's crust. It is a dark, sticky liquid containing only hydrogen and carbon **atoms** and is known as a **hydrocarbon**. After its extraction from the Earth, it is transported, usually in giant pipelines and oil tanker ships, to refineries. It is "cracked" or split into different parts, known as "fractions", and processed into a range of different fuels and raw materials that can be used for making chemicals and plastics.

Top world oil consumers, 2002	
Country	**Total oil consumption (million barrels per day)**
USA	20.0
China	5.6
Japan	5.4
Germany	2.6
Russia	2.6
India	2.2
South Korea	2.2
Canada	2.2
Brazil	2.1
France	2.1
Mexico	2.1

Source: World Oil 2003

Oil is the world's most important mineral resource, funding many countries' entire economies. It is used to generate electricity when burned, both at giant power stations, and as diesel fuel in small, local **generators**. Petrol or gasoline is the processed fraction of crude oil which powers over 600 million motor vehicles. Over 75 million barrels of oil per day are produced around the world by more than 40 nations. However, oil production is concentrated in a small number of nations including the USA, the UK, and many Middle East countries.

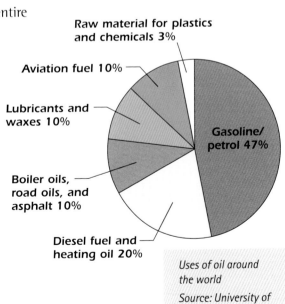

Raw material for plastics and chemicals 3%
Aviation fuel 10%
Lubricants and waxes 10%
Gasoline/petrol 47%
Boiler oils, road oils, and asphalt 10%
Diesel fuel and heating oil 20%

Uses of oil around the world
Source: University of Wisconsin, Milwaukee

13

Natural gas

Natural gas rises to the surface through natural openings in the Earth's crust, or can be brought to the surface through man-made wells on land or offshore. Humans discovered its uses for heating and lighting many centuries ago, but it was often regarded as a nuisance when encountered at oil wells and until as recently as 1980 was burned away in a process called "flaring off". In the past twenty years, natural gas use has grown more quickly than coal or oil. It can be used as a raw material for plastics and chemicals, and is burned in many power stations to generate electricity or is piped directly into homes for cooking and heating. Natural gas products such as liquid butane and propane are sold in steel cylinders as bottled gases for cooking stoves, heaters, and to run some machinery.

Dwindling reserves

The world's reliance on fossil fuels is a serious concern, as the reserves that remain will not last forever. Advances in technology and exploration mean that new fossil fuel fields and deposits are being discovered. For example, oil reserves actually increased by 12 per cent between 1993 and 2003, despite millions of barrels being used according to the Statistical Review of World Energy, 2004. However, few dispute the fact that fossil fuel reserves are slowly running out. It is estimated that natural gas reserves will last to the later decades of the 21st century or longer. Oil reserves may last for only between 40 and 50 years at current levels of use.

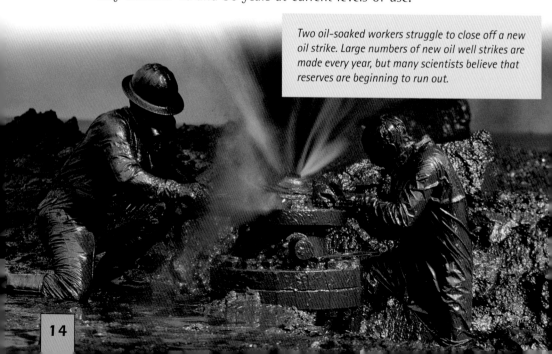

Two oil-soaked workers struggle to close off a new oil strike. Large numbers of new oil well strikes are made every year, but many scientists believe that reserves are beginning to run out.

Coal remains the most abundant of the fossil fuels, with scientists estimating that the known coal reserves would last over 210 years at the current rate of use. These reserves are mainly concentrated in a handful of countries: the USA (26 per cent), Russia and the other nations of the former Soviet Union (23 per cent), China (12 per cent), Australia (8 per cent), Germany (7 per cent) and South Africa (5 per cent).

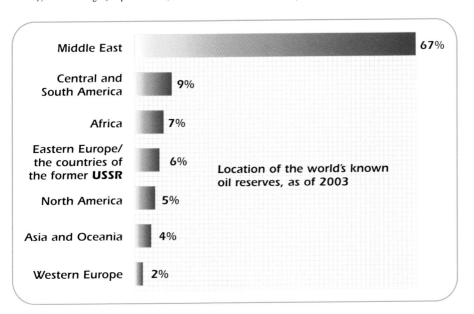

Location of the world's known oil reserves, as of 2003

Middle East	67%
Central and South America	9%
Africa	7%
Eastern Europe/ the countries of the former USSR	6%
North America	5%
Asia and Oceania	4%
Western Europe	2%

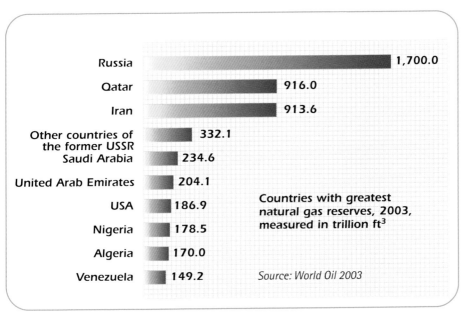

Countries with greatest natural gas reserves, 2003, measured in trillion ft³

Russia	1,700.0
Qatar	916.0
Iran	913.6
Other countries of the former USSR	332.1
Saudi Arabia	234.6
United Arab Emirates	204.1
USA	186.9
Nigeria	178.5
Algeria	170.0
Venezuela	149.2

Source: World Oil 2003

Nuclear energy

Most power stations burn fuel to create heat to generate electricity, but nuclear power stations are different. Instead of burning a fuel, they create heat by splitting the nuclei of atoms in a process called "**nuclear fission**". High-speed neutrons are fired at a metal called uranium. This breaks up the uranium nuclei and starts what is known as a "chain reaction". A vast amount of heat energy is produced by this process and can be used to drive electricity-generating **turbines**.

The first nuclear power station opened in 1956 and was based at Calder Hall in Cumbria, UK. Today, there are 440 commercial nuclear power reactors in operation in some 31 countries. The USA runs almost a quarter of these. India currently has plans for nine new nuclear power plants, Russia, four, and Japan, three.

NUCLEAR BENEFITS

When nuclear power was first introduced, many believed it would usher in a period of cheap energy for all. Nuclear power stations generate large amounts of energy from only small amounts of uranium-based fuel. The world reserves of uranium are estimated to last for at least 1,000 years and, possibly, much longer. Nuclear power produces no polluting smoke or carbon dioxide to contribute to **global warming**.

Nuclear fuel rods are kept underwater in a cooling pool at a nuclear power plant.

NUCLEAR FEARS

Radiation is a form of energy given off by certain substances. It is sometimes harmful and at high levels can cause cancers and death. In 1979, a small amount of radiation was released into the **atmosphere** at the Three Mile Island reactor in the US state of Pennsylvania. No one was harmed but public fears about nuclear power's safety increased even more after the major accident at Chernobyl, Ukraine, in 1986 (see case study on pages 30–31).

Nuclear power is reliable and theoretically cheap. However, its cost is greatly increased by the safety precautions that are taken to prevent harmful radioactivity escaping at power plants and reactors. In addition, there are major costs involved in dismantling old nuclear power stations – a process called "decommissioning". Although nuclear energy produces only a small amount of waste, what it does produce is highly radioactive and very dangerous. Exhausted or spent fuel rods containing uranium remain dangerously radioactive for between 500 and 1,000 years.

Proportion of electricity generated using nuclear power (1999)

France	78 per cent
Belgium	55 per cent
Sweden	50 per cent
South Korea	43 per cent
Switzerland	40 per cent
Japan	36 per cent
UK	29 per cent
Germany	28 per cent
USA	19 per cent
Hungary	11 per cent
Mexico	5 per cent

Source: WNI Jan 2005

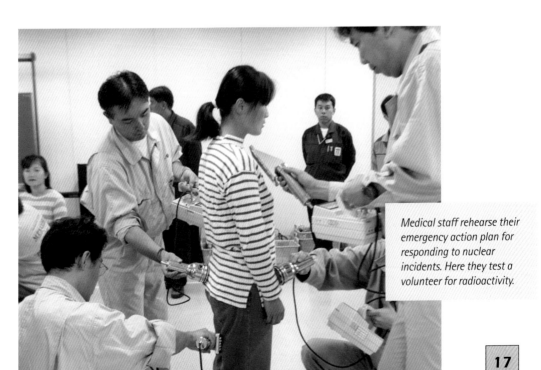

Medical staff rehearse their emergency action plan for responding to nuclear incidents. Here they test a volunteer for radioactivity.

Harnessing water energy

Moving water is a renewable energy source which has been harnessed by waterwheels and watermills since the times of the Ancient Greeks and Romans. Such devices are still used today to grind corn or spin yarn and cloth. Today, **hydroelectric power** (HEP) schemes are the most important renewable energy source and generate approximately one-fifth of the world's electricity.

The largest user of hydroelectric power is Canada, which gets about 62 per cent of its electricity from hydroelectric sources. Some mountainous countries, including Norway, Brazil, Democratic Republic of Congo, and Paraguay, use it to generate more than 80 per cent of their electricity. Some "micro-hydro" systems exist (see page 36) but the majority of electricity generated by hydroelectric power uses dams and reservoirs. Large schemes are expensive to build but are cheap to operate once constructed. They also generate no waste or air pollution. However, in recent years, concerns have grown about their environmental impact and how they remove **habitats** for types of living things and can affect water quality and quantity.

HARNESSING WAVES

Many different approaches are being researched and built to harness some of the large amount of energy in sea and ocean waves and to use it to drive electricity generators.

Attempts to transform the energy in sea and ocean waves in order to generate electricity include duck and buoy systems which float on the waves and use their up-and-down movement to turn turbines. Other systems funnel wave water through tubes to push air past turbines. Most wave power systems remain at the experimental stage currently and experts estimate that many kilometres of such machines would be needed to generate the power of one typical fossil fuel-run power station.

TIDAL BARRAGES

Tidal power works in a similar way to HEP schemes only the dam, known as a barrage, is much larger and is built across a river estuary – where the river meets the sea. As the tide goes in and out, water flows through tunnels in the barrage. This can generate electricity by turning turbines or pushing air through pipes. The largest tidal power barrage in the world is found at La Rance in France and was built in 1966. Only a small number of large barrages have been built since. Apart from their huge cost, tidal barrages can only be built in a small number of locations and only generate electricity when the tides are moving – this is approximately only a third of the time.

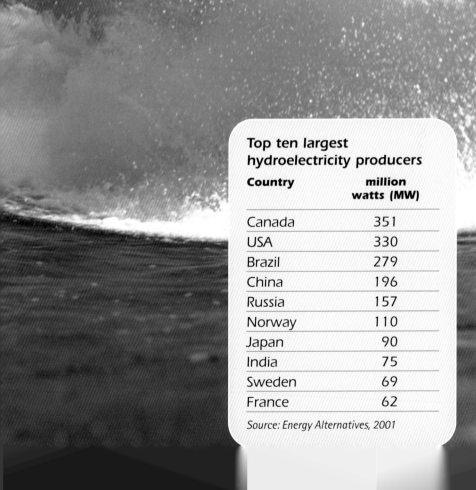

Top ten largest hydroelectricity producers

Country	million watts (MW)
Canada	351
USA	330
Brazil	279
China	196
Russia	157
Norway	110
Japan	90
India	75
Sweden	69
France	62

Source: Energy Alternatives, 2001

Energy from biomass

Any plant and animal matter that can be changed into energy is called "biomass". People have used biomass energy for thousands of years by burning wood, plants, and animal droppings. These sources of energy are still heavily used and are largely renewable, especially if tree stocks are replanted. Whilst biomass energy only forms a tiny part of the world's total commercial energy use (in industry and power stations), it is estimated to provide between 12 per cent and 16 per cent of the world's total energy use.

Top ten countries using traditional fuels (dung, plant matter, firewood) as a proportion of their total energy use

According to statistics from the World Bank, 49 countries rely on traditional fuels for a third or more of their total energy use.

Country	Percentage of biomass as total energy use
Chad	97.6
Eritrea	96.0
Ethiopia	95.9
Burundi	94.2
Cote d'Ivoire	91.5
Mozambique	91.4
Uganda	89.7
Nepal	89.6
Cambodia	89.3
Benin	89.2

Source: World Bank Development Indicators, 2002

Biomass energy can be harnessed to generate electricity or to create liquid and gas fuels for industry, cooking, heating, and motor vehicles. For example, in Brazil and elsewhere, sugar cane is fermented to make alcohol, which can be burned to generate electricity, or mixed with petrol to form "gasohol", a fuel for motor vehicles. The sugar cane can also be crushed to produce a pulp, called bagasse, which is then burned in power stations to generate electricity. Other energy crops include fast-growing trees, such as poplar and cottonwood. The rapeseed plant yields an oil, which when mixed with a type of alcohol, creates a diesel-type fuel used in some cars and power plants.

Fuel from animal droppings

In Suffolk, England, an advanced power station uses 160,000 tonnes of chicken litter – chicken manure, sawdust, and woods shavings – as its fuel. The power station generates 12.7 megawatts of electricity, enough to provide power for 22,000 homes.

Over 200 million people in India have no access to electricity. In many regions, animal dung is gathered by hand and left to dry in cakes or bricks (above). These are then burned to provide heat and cooking energy. Burning dung releases polluting substances such as carbon monoxide. Cooking in small rooms with little ventilation can, over time, cause breathing and heart diseases.

A device called a **biogas** digester, or "biodigester", offers an alternative use of animal and agricultural waste. It consists of a sealed container, 2 to 4 metres (6.5–13 feet) in diameter, into which dung and water are fed. The mixture ferments inside the container and eventually produces "biogas", made up of mainly methane and carbon dioxide. It can be piped into homes to be used as a cooking fuel, or used to fire a diesel engine to generate electricity. There are now 2.5 million of these devices in India. The waste sludge from the biodigester, known as slurry, makes an excellent fertilizer for farmland.

Harnessing the Sun, wind, and the Earth's heat

Since ancient times, energy from the Sun has been used to dry foods and animal skins and to bake clay bricks. Reflecting the sunlight onto a container is a method still used by many people in less developed nations to cook and warm food. Thermal or solar heaters are used as water heating systems in many countries including Greece, Australia, and in the US state of Hawaii, where more than 80,000 homes have such systems. These heaters concentrate the Sun's heat onto pipes and panels containing water.

Solar furnaces

Solar furnace heat can be used to generate electricity through steam-driven turbines or to purify water for drinking. Large numbers of mirrors are used to concentrate sunlight onto a solar furnace which drives up temperatures.

PHOTOVOLTAIC CELLS

Photovoltaic cells are electronic circuits which convert sunlight directly into electricity. A single cell produces only a tiny amount of electricity but useful amounts can be generated when cells are grouped together in panels. Large photovoltaic panels were fitted to the roofs of 665 houses in the athletes' village at the 2000 Sydney Olympics to provide these houses with electricity. Photovoltaic cells are non-polluting and are ideal for use in remote, sunny areas away from an electricity supply. But they do rely on a constant supply of sunshine, cannot work at night, and are relatively expensive.

WIND TURBINES

Wind can be harnessed to turn windmill or propeller-like turbines to generate electricity. On the Scottish island of Muck, for example, two 18-metre (59-feet) high turbines generate enough electricity to serve the island's 38-strong community. Often, the turbines are grouped in larger numbers in "wind farms" in areas where strong winds occur. A renewable and non-polluting energy source, the world total of wind turbines has doubled in the past eight years. In US states such as Montana and Texas, wind power generates enough electricity to supply over 1.5 million households. Denmark generates over 12 per cent of its total electricity in this way.

Top ten biggest wind energy producers, 2003

Country	Capacity (MW)
Germany	14,612
Spain	6,420
USA	6,361
Denmark	3,076
India	2,125
Netherlands	938
Italy	922
Japan	761
UK	759
China	571

Source: Envex 2004

GEOTHERMAL ENERGY PLANTS

Geothermal energy is the heat energy beneath the Earth's surface that creates hot springs and pools. Some of this energy can be tapped by drilling wells. Either the hot underground water is used for heating, or cold water is pumped down through the hot rocks and then recovered as superheated water and steam. It is sometimes used to generate electricity. More than 87 per cent of Iceland's homes are heated using geothermal energy. Plants also exist in a further 22 nations including the USA, Italy, New Zealand, Japan, and the Philippines.

Thermal springs provide the heat energy to fuel this power plant in Iceland, and keep the water warm enough for swimmers! In Iceland, over 80 per cent of homes are heated via thermal energy.

Energy impact and alternatives

All energy use has some form of cost or impact. Even a seemingly clean renewable energy such as solar photovoltaic cells have used up some other **resources**, such as raw materials and energy, in their manufacture. Many renewable energies, despite being less harmful to the environment, still have some negative impact. For example, geothermal power plants not only bring hot water to the surface but can also bring up minerals and gases including hydrogen sulphide, carbon dioxide, methane, and ammonia. Even wind farms can cause harm. Over a three-year period, over 100 birds of prey, including **endangered** golden eagles, were killed in the blades of the turbines at the Altamont Pass wind farm in California.

Fossil fuel impact

Extracting and using fossil fuels can have major impacts on environments. Large coalmines can strip away the land leaving it bare, waste from coal and oil can seep into rivers and lakes, and, as page 28 shows, oil leaks and slicks can harm coastal regions. However, the biggest impact of all comes from the pollution sent into the Earth's **atmosphere** by the burning of fossil fuels.

Average American car energy use and emissions per year

Distance travelled	20,125 km	(12,505 mi)
Fuel used	2,202 litres	(581 gal)
Hydrocarbons	34.7 kg	(76 lb)
Carbon monoxide	258.75 kg	(570 lb)
Nitrogen oxides	17.2 kg	(38 lb)
Carbon dioxide	5152.5 kg	(11,359 lb)

Source: United States Environmental Protection Agency

Air pollutants include carbon monoxide, sulphur dioxide, nitrogen oxides, and particulates – small particles of dust, soot, and smog. These pollutants are mainly caused by power plants and petrol-fuelled motor vehicles. In China, air pollution created by the burning of fossil fuels causes the deaths of approximately 500,000 people every year. The World Health Organisation estimates that air pollution causes three million deaths worldwide every year. Millions more suffer from air pollution-related diseases, particularly breathing disorders such as asthma, bronchitis, and pneumonia.

What causes acid rain?

Acid rain is a form of pollution where rain, snow, sleet, or hail is polluted by acid in the atmosphere, and eventually falls, damaging the environment. Two air pollutants, sulphur dioxide and nitrogen oxides, are the main causes of acid rain. Most sulphur dioxide enters the atmosphere from coal-burning industries and electricity power stations. Nitrogen oxides in the atmosphere come also from burning fossil fuels in industry, in electricity generation, and in motor vehicles.

Acid rain is often carried on winds and falls great distances from where it began. For example, 90 per cent of the acid rain which falls on Norway comes from outside its borders. Acid rain can be devastating to the environment, killing trees and poisoning lakes. Eastern North America, China, and Europe are amongst the hardest-hit areas. In Poland, 40 per cent of the trees in many of its forests are already dead or dying.

What is the "enhanced greenhouse effect"?

Gases, such as carbon dioxide and methane, are found naturally in the Earth's atmosphere and are known as **greenhouse gases**. This is because they perform an important job, trapping some of the Sun's energy as heat and helping to warm the planet's surface. This is called the "greenhouse effect". But since the middle of the 18th century, when industries started to develop greatly and energy use rose, levels of these gases in the atmosphere have risen by as much as 32 per cent. The main causes are believed to be the burning of fossil fuels in industry and motor vehicles, and the cutting down of much of the world's forests. According to many scientists, the result of these increased levels of gases is that more heat is trapped, causing global warming (the phenomenon of increasing global temperatures). This is known as the "enhanced greenhouse effect".

Global warming is a complex process and no one is exactly certain what will occur in the future. However, the warmest ten years on record have all occurred since 1990, and most scientists believe that global temperatures are likely to increase by 1 to 5 °C (2 to 9 °F) by the end of this century. This could lead to a great increase in droughts and floods, with many farmlands being unable to support crops, and a rise in infectious disease. The Intergovernmental Panel on **Climate** Change reports that sea levels could rise by over 30 centimetres (12 inches) by the 22nd century. This would result in huge areas of land being submerged. The US Environmental Protection Agency (EPA) estimates that as much as 58,000 square kilometres (22,393 square miles) of the USA's eastern coastline could be under threat, including parts of the cities of Boston, New York, Charleston, Miami, and New Orleans. This is just a tiny fraction of the total land around the world threatened by rises in sea level.

Carbon dioxide levels

Over 22 million tonnes of carbon dioxide is sent into the atmosphere every year through the world's use of fossil fuels. Electricity generation is one of the biggest culprits. According to energy analysts, The Cadmus Group, an average of 7.4 kilograms (16.4 pounds) of carbon dioxide is sent into the atmosphere for every 10 kilowatt hours of electricity generated.

World carbon dioxide emissions from fossil fuel use

Just eight countries were responsible in 1999 for almost half of the world's carbon dioxide emissions.

Country	CO_2 (millions of tonnes)	Percentage of world emissions
USA	5,578	24.7
Russia	1,468.3	6.5
Japan	1,125.4	5
Germany	843.8	3.7
UK	559.3	2.5
Canada	553.8	2.5
Italy	445.1	2
France	398.5	1.8
World total	**22,547.1**	**100**

Source: US Energy Information Administration

Increased carbon dioxide emissions are thought to be contributing to global warming. An increase in world temperatures may lead to changes in agricultural production.

Is transporting fuels for energy safe?

Hundreds of thousands of journeys transporting fuels by ship, road, rail, or pipeline are completed safely every year. Public fears often focus on the moving of radioactive fuel and waste to and from nuclear power and reprocessing plants, although there have been no major accidents involving the transport of nuclear materials. However, accidents have occurred transporting oil, with pipeline leaks as well as oil spills from tankers.

The *Exxon Valdez*

In 1989, the *Exxon Valdez* oil tanker ran aground on a reef some 65 kilometres (40 miles) off the coast of the US state of Alaska. The tanker leaked 38,800 tonnes of crude oil into the waters along an estimated 2,080 kilometres (1,290 miles) of the coast of Alaska. Clean-up operations lasted four years, but an estimated spend of US$2,100 million could not save the lives of around 250,000 seabirds, 2,800 sea otters, 300 harbour seals, and millions of salmon and herring eggs and their young. Coastal communities were severely affected by the oil spill, and fifteen years later, not all the region's species of fish and birds have recovered.

Dangerous industries

Obtaining energy sources and working with them can be hazardous. Many of the energy sources are easily **combustible**, and fires and explosions are a serious risk. The most severe accident involving natural gas occurred in the Cleveland, USA, in 1944. Liquid natural gas leaked from a storage plant, formed a cloud of gas, and then ignited and burned, killing 128 people. In January 2004, a similar leak and explosion at the Skikda plant in Algeria claimed the lives of 27 people.

In the North Sea oilfields, where reserves are mainly owned by the UK and Norway, there have been 400 deaths since 1969. Some fear that as reserves of valuable oil and coal dwindle, companies will be forced to take fossil fuels from increasingly dangerous locations. This will put workers at greater risk, especially those in countries where health and safety levels are not as strict as elsewhere.

The worst North Sea oilfield accident occurred in 1988 when the Piper Alpha oil platform, southeast of the Orkney Islands, caught fire. 167 people died as a result.

The legacy of Chernobyl

In 1986, disaster struck the Chernobyl nuclear plant, 104 kilometres (65 miles) north of Kiev (then in the USSR, now in the Ukraine). Reactor number 4 exploded, caught fire and, according to the World Health Organization, released a large amount of radioactive material into the atmosphere. This radioactive material was 400 times more than was released by the atomic bomb dropped on Hiroshima, Japan in World War II. Winds dispersed the material across much of Europe and into the UK. Small amounts of radiation even reached North America.

An area of at least 150,000 square kilometres (57,915 square miles) was contaminated in Belarus, Russia, and the Ukraine, and over 200,000 people were evacuated, never to return to their homes. Studies have since shown higher levels of cancers and other health problems in people from the region. In addition, large areas of farmland have been ruined. The financial costs of the Chernobyl disaster have been huge. According to the Chernobyl Children's Project, the economic damage to Belarus over 30 years (1986–2015) will be US$235,000 million. The remains of the radioactive reactor lie entombed in a concrete and steel casing which is beginning to crumble. A new structure is expected to be put in place by 2010 at an estimated cost of £1,000,000,000 (US$1,760,000,000).

What you can do to reduce carbon dioxide emissions

- Unplug mobile phone chargers when not in use. A mobile phone charger plugged in permanently over a year can use electricity which takes 35 to 70 kilograms (77–154 pounds) of carbon dioxide emissions to produce.
- Hang clothes out to dry rather than use an electric clothes drier. The electricity used for an average tumble dry is equivalent to around 1.5 kilograms (3.3 pounds) of carbon dioxide emissions.
- Encourage your local school and community groups to plant new trees. Trees absorb carbon dioxide.

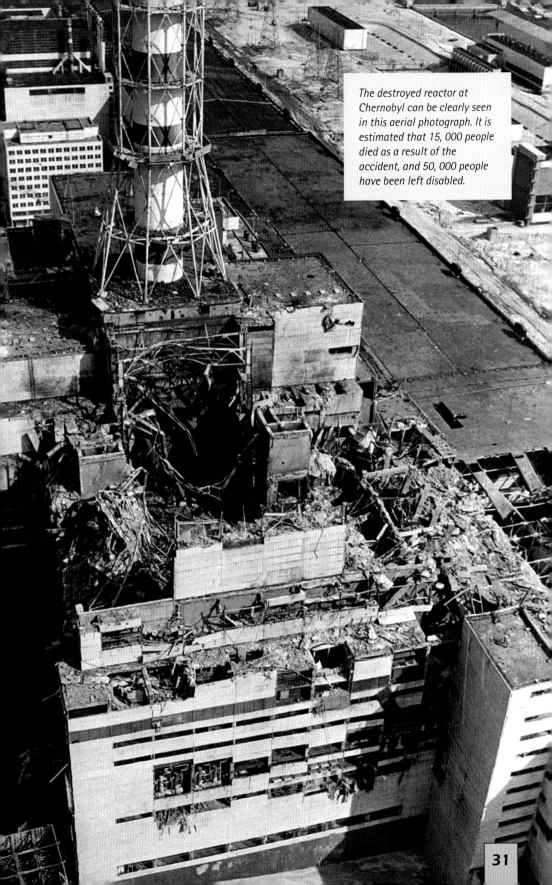

The destroyed reactor at Chernobyl can be clearly seen in this aerial photograph. It is estimated that 15, 000 people died as a result of the accident, and 50, 000 people have been left disabled.

Seeking solutions

With reserves of some energy sources dwindling, rising pollution, and concerns about global warming, many people believe that changes are vital to safeguard the planet and the life it supports. But achieving change can be very difficult.

All energy production comes at a cost. Even when the energy source appears to be free, such as the Sun's rays or the planet's winds, there are large costs in developing and building the technology to use and transport it. A single 500-kilowatt wind **turbine**, for example, may cost over £300,000 (US$527,000) and many may be needed to supply a medium-sized community with electricity. **Fossil fuels** dominate energy use across the world. Changing from fossil fuels to another system, such as **renewable energy** sources, can cost large sums – money which many energy companies and governments have been reluctant to spend.

The Kyoto Protocol and cutting emissions

Over 140 countries made an international agreement in 1997, known as the Kyoto Protocol, which set targets for nations to cut their emissions of **greenhouse gases.** One important way to achieve cuts in emissions is to switch from fossil fuels to renewable energies. These have many benefits yet still form only a tiny fraction of most countries' energy use. In the USA, for instance, only 6.5 per cent of all energy consumed is from renewable sources. In the UK, less than 2 per cent of all energy comes from renewable energy sources. The UK is part of the European Union (EU) which has set a target of 12 per cent of all total energy to come from renewable energy sources by 2010.

The Kyoto Protocol came into force in 2005. A symposium was held in Japan to commemorate the event and to discuss further measures.

Building new energy facilities often arouses conflict and protests from different groups with different views. Many people, for example, like the idea of renewable energy sources, such as wind power, but are less enthusiastic about a collection of wind turbines being sited near their homes. They claim it spoils their area and generates noise pollution, even though noise is relatively minimal and the land underneath turbines can still be used for farming.

UK renewable energy sources, 2003

Biofuels and waste	87.3 per cent
Large-scale HEP	8.3 per cent
Wind	3.4 per cent
Geothermal and active solar heating	0.7 per cent
Small-scale HEP	0.3 per cent

Source: UK Department of Trade and Industry

Sites suitable for some renewable energies, such as geothermal energy, are often found in areas of great natural beauty or inside national parks or protected areas. This can cause concern amongst ecologists who fear disruption to the **habitats** of plants and creatures. Most geothermal power plants will require a large amount of water for cooling or other purposes. In places where water is in short supply, this need could raise conflicts with other users for water resources.

The Three Gorges Dam

The greatest impact of renewable energy sources comes with large-scale hydroelectric power schemes which dam rivers, submerging land to form a giant reservoir.

The building of what will be the world's most powerful hydroelectric power plant on the Yangtze River in China has provoked intense debate. The 26 giant turbines at the Three Gorges Dam at Sandouping will generate 18,200 megawatts (18 million kilowatts) of electricity. This is almost one-tenth of the whole of China's electrical output. Yet, this project comes with significant costs to the **economy** and environment, as the following table illustrates.

Issue	Against	For
Cost	The dam is expensive. The cost of building the dam could soar to as much as US$75,000 million.	The dam is currently within budget at US$25,000 million and will provide the same amount of electricity as 18 nuclear power plants.
Local human impact	Between 1.1 and 2 million people will be forced to resettle away from their homelands.	15 million people downstream will be better off due to regular electricity and control of floods which damage the region.
Environment	Water pollution and deforestation will increase, and many species of plants and animals will become endangered.	China has high air pollution levels from burning coal. Hydroelectric power causes little air pollution. The dam will provide the same energy as burning 50 million tonnes of coal.
Local culture and natural beauty	The 600 km (373 miles) long reservoir will flood 1,300 archaeological and historic sites and damage the tourism industry.	Many archaeological and historical relics are being moved.
Navigation	The slower river will deposit millions of tonnes of silt and clog ports and harbours in a few years.	Shipping will become faster, cheaper, and safer as the dam will slow river waters and let ships pass through locks.

Energy for all?

Energy use is not shared equally amongst all people of the world. Accord
to figures from the United Nations (UN), the world's richest people use
around 25 times more energy per person than the world's poorest. Just 2
per cent of the world's people consume more than 65 per cent of the
world's energy. Some more developed countries want all nations to use
cleaner, safer energy, and take more care of the environment. But for mo
of the poorer nations, where people struggle for any form of energy alon
with food and water, the long-term health of the environment is not the
biggest concern. To many people, the responsibility lies with the wealthie
nations in two important ways. Firstly, they must find ways to use more
renewable energy and to halt or reduce their own enormous energy
consumption. And secondly, they should develop and fund ways in which
renewable energy can be supplied and made affordable to countries
not as wealthy as they are.

Micro-hydro renewable energy in Kenya

In the UK, over 97 per cent of the population have access to mains electricity,
supplied by the electricity grid. In the African nation of Kenya, 96 per cent
of people live without access. Desperately poor families may be forced to
spend a third of their limited income on expensive kerosene and diesel fuels

to mill grain, and light and power their
homes. HEP might provide a solution.
Much smaller plants called micro-hydro
power plants that do not require a dam
can provide local communities with
much-needed electricity and have far
less impact on the environment. The
Tungu-Kabri Micro-hydro Power Project,
for example, in the Kenyan village of
Mbuirunow, provides energy for 1,000
people. This enables them to start small
businesses, spend less of their income
on expensive fuels, become connected
to the outside world through electronic
media (left), and help themselves to
fight poverty.

The Honda fuel cell car

In 2002, following many years of research, Japanese car-makers, Honda, began to sell models of its FCX car. The car is powered by electricity which is generated within the vehicle by a **fuel cell**. The fuel cell generates electricity by combining hydrogen from its tank with oxygen taken in from the air. Remarkably, the only emission from the car, which has a range of up to 354 kilometres (220 miles) and a top speed of 144 kmph (90 mph), is water.

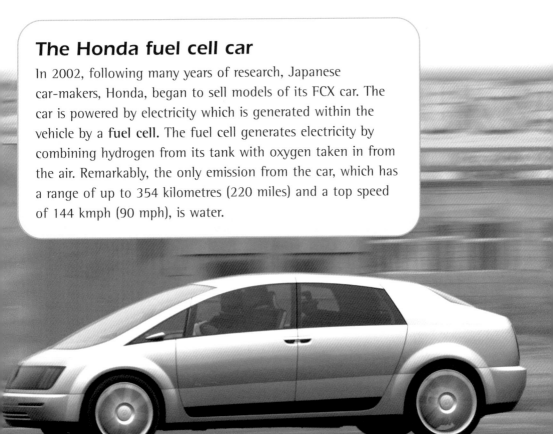

Energy innovations

Whilst local, renewable energy can help small communities, researchers are trying to develop renewable alternatives to the big energy users in large towns and cities. These include the lighting of buildings and transportation which uses one quarter of the world's energy, mostly fossil fuels.

One alternative to fossil fuels that is being developed is hydrogen. This gas is only found in combination with other elements, such as oxygen in water. Fuel cells are devices that directly convert hydrogen into electricity. They can be used to generate electricity. They were first used by NASA in their space programme to power electrical items, provide heat, and purify drinking water. Hydrogen-based fuel cells offer many advantages. Hydrogen is abundant, high in energy, and yet, when burned, produces almost zero pollution.

At present, fuel cells and the technology to separate hydrogen from other elements is expensive. But experts argue that costs would fall dramatically if the units were mass-produced.

Saving energy

Some solutions and improvements require the agreement of governments and industries and are very expensive. Yet, individuals can make a difference through many important actions at little or no cost. There are many ways to save energy. For example, low energy light bulbs can save more than 60 per cent on a household's lighting bill. Individuals and households can simply use less energy by not using certain electrical items as often, such as hairdryers, fan heaters, and air conditioners, or switching off and unplugging electrical items when not in use. They can arrange car sharing or use their motor vehicles less, choosing instead to cycle, walk, or opt for public transport.

Every car journey under 4.9 kilometres (3 miles) avoided saves enough energy to prevent around 2 kilograms (4.4 pounds) of carbon dioxide being sent into the atmosphere. Cutting down car use also saves money. Walking 6 kilometres (3.7 miles) each day, such as a 3-kilometre (1.8-mile) trip to and from school, could save over £200 (US$350) per year. Large energy savings can also be made by people consuming less products, reusing items such as containers and carry bags, and **recycling** waste items.

What you can do to save energy
- Arrange car sharing when taking trips with friends.
- Walk or use a bicycle for short journeys, rather than a car.
- Only use washing machines and dishwashers with a full load.
- Reuse carry bags and containers, rather than buying new ones.
- Recycle waste objects such as glass, paper, and aluminium drink cans.

Improving energy efficiency

Improving energy efficiency means making each unit of energy used produce more work. Through research by companies, many products have become much more energy efficient than in the past. For example, in the USA, the amount of electricity needed to run a fridge which has passed the Energy Star efficiency programme, is around half that of fridges in 1993. By replacing devices such as water heaters, fridges, and air conditioning systems with more energy-efficient devices, and by improving home **insulation** to hold in heat more efficiently, households can save much energy.

Compact Fluorescent Light Bulbs

There are now energy-saving light bulbs, called Compact Fluorescent Light bulbs (CFLs). If every US household fitted five of these bulbs in place of their most used lights, the energy saved would be equal to the yearly output of 21 power plants. Approximately 450 million tonnes of greenhouse gas emissions would not occur.

Although they cost around £5 each, CFL bulbs last between 6 and 10 times longer than a regular light bulb, whilst using two thirds less energy.

Tomorrow's energy, tomorrow's issues

As the population of the world increases, more and more countries seek to develop and build new industries. They want better standards of living for their people, so the demand for energy will continue to grow. The US Department of Energy predicts that world energy consumption will increase by at least 60 per cent by 2020. Much of the growth in energy use is expected to be in developing nations, particularly in Asia and in Central and South America, where energy demand is expected to double over the next twenty years.

China's increasing drivers

As China's industries have developed, more and more Chinese people are buying motor vehicles. In 2003, approximately 11,000 new cars hit the roads every single day, a total of 4 million new private cars. If this growth continues, experts predict that more than 150 million cars will be on China's roads by 2016. That is 10 million cars more than are now found in the USA.

With increasing demand comes the likelihood of increasing problems, including **global warming**, environmental impact, and an energy gap between those who can afford energy and those who cannot. Increasing energy efficiency, recycling, and reducing consumption waste and pollution, will all be essential for people and the planet to flourish.

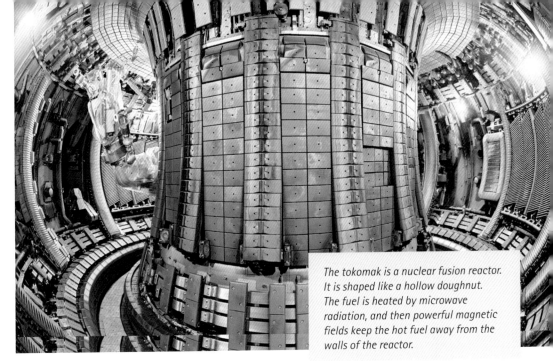

The tokomak is a nuclear fusion reactor. It is shaped like a hollow doughnut. The fuel is heated by microwave radiation, and then powerful magnetic fields keep the hot fuel away from the walls of the reactor.

Future energies

Future energy breakthroughs in areas such as hydrogen power and **nuclear fusion** may provide alternatives to **fossil fuels**. Where **nuclear fission** splits the nuclei of atoms, nuclear fusion forces nuclei to join together. Nuclear fusion is how the sun generates its vast amounts of energy. It would generate far less **radioactive** waste and be safer than nuclear fission.

Other research is centring on using deuterium, obtainable from seawater, as a fuel. A thimble full of deuterium would generate the same amount of energy as 20 tonnes of coal.

Energy predictions for 2025

- World population to rise from 6,400 million to 8,200–8,600 million
- World electricity demand to almost double
- Carbon dioxide emissions up over 60 per cent to 37,000 million tonnes per year
- Natural gas use to double on 2001 levels to 31,200 million barrels
- Number of motor vehicles on the world's roads to exceed 1,000 million
- Nuclear power use to drop in more developed countries, but to rise in less developed nations
- Renewable energy use to rise but still far behind use of fossil fuels.

Sources: International Energy Outlook, World Energy Outlook

Statistical information

Percentage of world energy consumed by various countries, against their population as a percentage of the world's population.

Country	Percentage of world energy consumed	Percentage of world population
USA	25	4.6
China	9.9	21.2
Russia	7	2.5
Japan	5.8	2.1
Germany	3.9	1.3
India	3.1	16.6
France	2.9	0.9
UK	2.6	1
Canada	2.5	0.5
Korea	1.9	0.7

Wealthy industralized countries consume a far higher proportion of the world's energy, against population, than less developed countries.

Top 20 oil producing countries, 2002

Country	Millions of barrels per day
Saudi Arabia	8.528
USA	8.091
Russia	7.014
Iran	3.775
Mexico	3.560
Norway	3.408
China	3.297
Venezuela	3.137
Canada	2.749
United Arab Emirates	2.550
UK	2.540
Iraq	2.377
Nigeria	2.223
Kuwait	1.838
Brazil	1.589
Algeria	1.486
Libya	1.427
Indonesia	1.384
Oman	0.964
Argentina	0.825

Top 20 net oil importers by estimated barrels per day (2002)

Country	Barrels per day
USA	10.4 million
Japan	5.3 million
Germany	2.6 million
France	1.85 million
Italy	1.69 million
China	1.6 million*
Spain	1.5 million
India	1.2 million
Turkey	584,326
Thailand	539,973*
Guatemala	427,000*
Greece	397,008*
Philippines	347,540*
Pakistan	312,000
Israel	273,000
South Africa	258,000*
Ukraine	254,500*
Australia	239,082*
Bangladesh	68,800
Panama	57,000*

*2001 estimates.
Source: US Department of Energy

World-predicted energy consumption in quadrillion BTU, where 1 quadrillion BTU = 25 million tonnes of oil equivalent

Region	1990	2001	2010	2025
Industrialized countries	182.8	211.5	236.3	281.4
Eastern Europe and former Soviet Union	76.3	53.3	59.0	75.6
Developing countries	89.3	139.2	175.5	265.9
Asia	52.5	85.0	110.6	173.4
Middle East	13.1	20.8	25.0	34.1
Africa	9.3	12.4	14.6	21.5
Central and South America	14.4	20.9	25.4	36.9
Total world	348.4	403.9	470.8	622.9

Source: Energy Information Administration, Department of Energy, USA

U.S. energy consumption by source (in quadrillion BTU)

Year	Oil	Gas	Coal	Nuclear	Other	Total
1980	34.20	20.39	15.39	2.74	11.42	84.14
2004	40.82	25.59	23.82	7.89	7.49	105.61

Source: Energy Information Administration

A quadrillion BTU is a huge measure of energy. To put this into perspective, world energy consumption in 2001 was 404 quadrillion BTU.

UK energy consumption (in millions of tonnes of oil equivalent)

Fuel	1980	2003
Oil	76.2	74.1
Coal	73.3	40.4
Gas	44.8	94.5
Renewables and waste	less than 1	3.2
Nuclear	10.2	20.6

Source: UK Department of Trade and Industry

Glossary

atmosphere collection of gases that surround Earth

atom smallest unit of matter that can take part in a chemical reaction

barrel unit of measure of oil which is equal to 42 US gallons or 159 litres

biofuel fuel that comes from biomass – living material such as wood

biogas type of gas, rich in methane, produced using animal dung, human sewage, or crops in an air-tight container. Biogas can be used as a fuel to generate electricity, or burned to generate heat.

climate general weather conditions of a region or the entire Earth over a long period of time

combustible easily catches fire

deforestation cutting down of large numbers of trees for fuel or timber, or to clear the land for settlements or farming

economy way in which natural resources are used and goods and services are produced, distributed (sold or passed on to people), and consumed (used by organizations or people)

emission gases, water vapour, and particulate (soot) released into the air by fires, industry, and other human activity. Some emissions are extremely harmful.

endangered species species of living thing which are seriously threatened with dying out

fossil fuel material which can be burned to generate energy. It was formed from living material which has decayed and been buried in the ground for millions of years.

fuel cell device which converts chemical energy into electrical energy and usually uses hydrogen as a fuel

generator device which produces electrical energy from mechanical energy

global warming warming-up of the Earth's surface due to changes in the gases which form the Earth's atmosphere

greenhouse gas mixed gases in the atmosphere that trap heat from the Sun and warm the Earth

habitat surroundings that a particular species needs to survive. Habitats include coral reefs, grasslands, freshwater lakes, and deserts. Some creatures can live in more than one habitat.

hydrocarbon substance made up solely of carbon and hydrogen atoms

hydroelectric power system for generating electricity by using the power of falling water to turn turbines linked to an electricity generator

industrialized/industrialization process in which more and more emphasis is placed upon industry and manufacturing in a country's economy

insulation material or device which stops the travel of heat or electricity

kilowatt-hour (kWh) one kilowatt-hour is a measure of energy used by many electricity companies. It is equal to the energy expended by 1,000 watts in an hour.

natural gas mixture of methane and other gases found underground or below the seabed which can be used as a fuel

nuclear fission splitting apart of the nuclei of atoms to generate energy

nuclear fusion joining or fusing together of nuclei of atoms to generate energy

ore type of mineral which contains useful metals such as iron, copper, or zinc which can be extracted

photovoltaic cell device that converts energy from light into electrical energy

pollution waste products or heat which damages the environment in some way

radiation/radioactivity harmful rays and particles given off by certain substances as their atoms split apart

recycling recovering waste material to make new products. Can also mean to re-use discarded products.

renewable energy energy from a source which can be restored and maintained. Wind and solar energy are both examples of renewable energies.

resources natural things found on Earth such as metals, trees, coal, or water which can be used in some way

solar power power obtained from the energy of the Sun's rays

turbine a device for transforming energy from moving water, steam, or wind into mechanical energy which can drive a generator to produce electricity

USSR Union of Soviet Socialist Republics

Further Reading

Books

Brown, Paul. *Energy and Resources* (Watts, 2000)
This book looks at the demands of a growing world population and the pressures it places on the Earth's energy resources.

Collinson, Alan. *Renewable Energy* (Evans Brothers, 1997)
Here you can find a detailed, clear look at the technologies behind alternative energy sources.

Donnellan, Craig. Ed. *The Energy Debate* (Independence Educational Publishers, 2001)
The debate comprises a fascinating collection of reports, letters, and news stories concerned with the issues of energy use and efficiency.

Parker, Steve. *Fuels for the Future* (Wayland, 1997)
Use this title for a good overview and guide to the issues facing different forms of energy sources.

Snedden, Robert. *Energy Alternatives* (Heineman, 2001)
This book looks at different types of energy such as solar, wind, and hydroelectric power, which can act as alternatives to fossil fuels and nuclear power.

An adult can help you with the following books:

Brown, Lester. *The State of the World 2004* (Worldwatch Institute, 2004)
This is an important, annual guide to the world, its people, and its resources with charts and up-to-date statistics files on energy, consumption, and resources.

Clayton, Caroline. *Dirty Planet* (Friends of the Earth/Livewire Publishing, 2000)
This is an adult book, but written in plain, easy-to-understand English. It looks at practical ways for individuals and communities to make a difference in their use of energy. It also discusses how to reduce pollution.

Cothran, Helen, Ed. *Energy Alternatives* (Greenhaven Press, 2002)
Here you can read a collection of thought-provoking reports and essays about energy issues from different points of view.

Websites

California Energy Commission

http://www.energyquest.ca.gov/index.html
A fascinating and fun site, here you can find large amounts of up-to-date information on energy use, conservation, and new technologies, such as motor vehicles run on alternative fuels.

Greenpeace

http://www.greenpeace.org
This international organization promotes environmental awareness and understanding. It has comprehensive news and report sections on nuclear power and climate change.

International Energy Agency

http://www.iea.org/textbase/subjectqueries/index.asp
Search the massive database of reports and fact files on this website.

Addresses

American Petroleum Institute (API)
1220 L St. NW
Washington DC
20005
USA
Tel: (202) 682 8000

American Solar Energy Society
(ASES)
2400 Central Avenue, Suite G-1,
Boulder
Colorado 80301
USA

Geothermal Education Office (GEO)
664 Hilary Drive
Tiburon
California 94920
USA
Tel: (415) 435 4574

Friends of The Earth
26–28 Underwood Street
London
N1 7JQ
UK

INDEX

Titles in the *Planet Under Pressure* series include:

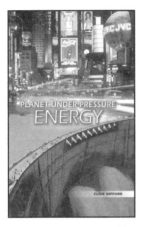

Hardback: 1-844-43978-X

Hardback: 1-844-43979-8

Hardback: 1-844-43974-7

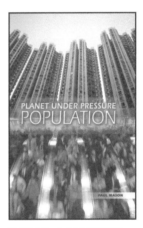

Hardback: 1-844-43977-1

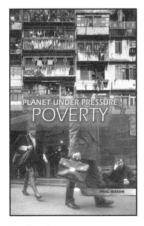

Hardback: 1-844-43975-5

Hardback: 1-844-43976-3

Find out about other titles from Raintree on our website www.raintreepublishers.co.uk